Extraordinary Encounters

By

Francis McDonnell

Published in 2024

By

Kindle Direct Publishing

About the Author/This Collection

I was born in London but have lived in Luton for most of my life, going to Stockwood High School and Luton Sixth Form College before going to the University of Bath for a BSc in Mathematics. Subsequent activity includes three-and-a-half years working as a Mathematician in Cheltenham before studying for a Ph.D. in Operational Research at Loughborough University. My main activity at present is as a Mathematician. Interests include walking and art as well as, of course, writing poetry and occasionally prose.

I started writing poems more frequently and became an active member of Luton Poetry Society (L.P.S.) in 2013. I enjoy writing and performing poetry that rhymes, has a matching number of syllables and sometimes even has, in parts, a tolerable meter. In this collection only two of the nineteen poems do not rhyme. My favourite poets are John Betjeman, Pam Ayres, John Cooper Clarke, John Hegley, Roger McGough and Benjamin Zephaniah. I think there are some important connections between mathematics and poetry and have even performed a poem at a Luton Poetry Society meeting describing some of them. More recently I have been a member of Poetry ID and Wardown Poets. The painting on the front cover was by me.

Acknowledgements

Some of the poems in this collection were written for performance at Wardown Poets. I thank the members of Wardown Poets for providing a new poetic stimulus and audience for some of my poems, especially Barrie Kemp for his part in running it.

I also thank my friends and family for their support over the period during which these poems were written.

To Larry Jackson

Contents

A Lodger

4.12.23

An Indian lodger arrived one day

Helped by two male friends, she had come to stay

Both young and pretty she looked very kind

She said something that puzzled my mind

She asked if I would stay with her till five

I thought with her friends there she would thrive

So I politely declined her invite

And went back to my home to stay the night

Alas for her, her friends left her alone

Which took her out of her comfort zone

For she had wanted constant company

When we met, that's something I didn't see

When I then learned of her enormous need

A part of me wanted to then take heed

And be with her so she wasn't lonely

A delicate flower should be nurtured, only

I had a cold I wanted not to pass on

And within just a week she had gone

Despite the other lodgers there

Perhaps they didn't seem to care

I might have taken her out for some tea

But now that she's gone it may never be

A Man in a Red Suit

29.11.23

In Luton Library one sunny day

A fairly young black man made a display

On level two where the study is quiet

He wore a red suit, now where did he buy it?

Most probably from on the internet

As around here it would be hard to get

The jacket and trousers matched perfectly

It really was quite a sight to see

A departure from the murky norm

Of the black and dull blue uniform

Most boldly he was going his own way

I wonder if I'll see it again some day

Meanwhile I enjoy my red winter coat

For a bit of colour gets my vote

A Man in Berlin

16.1.24

Berlin, Brandenberg and Warsaw were seen

By my brothers and I, and a man was keen

Whilst on the tube, to show us around

His generosity did us astound

He showed us lots of the sights of Berlin

He said for the BBC he was working

He said that he'd be in our hotel bar

In the evening so we needn't go far

But so extremely taken aback were we

By unbelievable generosity

That we wondered if we could trust the man

And omitting the bar was then our plan

But the encounter was memorable

And gave one a tale that seemed very tall

A Man with Balls

29.11.23

Whilst walking along The Mall years ago
I came across a very strange fellow
Middle-aged, bald and wearing a robe
He seemed influenced by elsewhere on the globe
He carried four balls with two on each palm
And though rather odd he seemed very calm
He held out his hands like gifts to the world
And around and around the balls he swirled

Slowly along The Mall he processed
Maybe with him some were obsessed
Such a character, so eccentric
Maybe someone wanted to take a pic
Then perhaps about him a movie make
And bring it out soon for morale's sake

A Young Beggar

26.11.23

A Romanian beggar years ago

Begged people for cash as they went to and fro

Out in the open on Luton's main street

Right next to Don Miller's he kept his beat

Young with brown hair and a tooth of gold

He fed family from work in the cold

I sometimes in sympathy gave him cash

I did not think I was being rash

But once he had learned that I had a heart

When I passed near him from his place he'd dart

Right across the other side of the street

Hoping for money from me to entreat

I haven't seen him for many years now

Is he poor, dead, or with shares in the Dow?

Hopefully he is not in despair,

Has a job, and lives in comfort somewhere

An Old Beggar

27.11.23

A man who looked like he was past fifty

And was as polite as he could be

With grey hair and beard he seemed very nice

And one supposed that he did not have vice

He sat on the ground near the old railway

That went off to Dunstable in its day

I have no idea where it was he slept

But quite respectable-looking he kept

I gave him some coins a couple of times

Feeling sorry for him in these climes

Going to Bury Park supermarkets

Thinking that he wouldn't use it for bets

For ages I didn't come across him

Our chances of meeting seemed to be slim

But I recently saw him on a bike

So maybe his earnings had had a spike –

Upward mobility observed for real

As he slowly revolved each bicycle wheel

17

Ashton Stores Staff

1.1.24

My nearest shop is Ashton Stores

And though old hat, it never bores

For there's variety in drinks

And though no staff there ever winks

I've chatted with a fair number

And though not good for a cucumber

They are quite good for a newspaper

And though I've never been a vaper

They do sell lots of tobacco

Though of course you reap what you sow

The highlight though has been a student

A Masters one who thought it prudent

To work there for a little while

I hope one day he makes a pile

His course was mainly computing

Nerdy and mild, we liked talking

I think that now he has moved on

It's not the same since he has gone

Ben Nevis Helper

17.1.24

On a Holiday Fellowship Holiday

Based in Fort William on a summer's day

We went to climb Ben Nevis the hard way

There was a tricky moment I must say

Whilst climbing a rock face, at the group's rear

I couldn't make progress and felt some fear

But a helpful man twenty years older

Helped me choose my grip on the next boulder

I'd been stuck and he may have saved my life

We descended the easy way for less strife

And so I lived to tackle many things new

To that man I would like to say "Thank you"

Not knowing his name, perhaps I should strive

To ring up the programme "Saturday Live"!

Encounter with Genius/Madness (An extended tanka)

10.3.24

A genius has

a mind like Bluebeard's Castle,

with troubling doors locked

during their early childhood.

Some doors open up great rooms

and they are played in,

but life can be difficult

and sometimes stressful.

Stress may unlock all the doors.

The restless mind opens some.

Troubled by what's there,

madness may quickly ensue,

and tablets taken;

the lively wing's then blocked off

and thoughts confined to the rest.

Taper the tablets

and the wing will reopen!

If reduced too much,

split the difference between

what's too much and too little.

Keep splitting until

you find the optimum dose.

Occasionally

troubling doors will be opened –

you should shut them straight away.

Dismiss their contents!

Move on to wonderful rooms

and stay there a while

to achieve your potential,

or at least something quite close.

'Mrs Pepperpot'

24.1.24

A woman of perhaps late middle age

Who probably wasn't earning a wage

Used to walk slowly along my road

Stopping often in a very strange mode

A few short steps, then stop and repeat

But her appearance was remarkably neat

She wore a nice coat, handbag and hat

And what I recall amounts to just that

I expect she had health problems unknown

And maybe by now to heaven she's flown

For I haven't seen her in many a year

Though all this while I have stayed around here

Sainsbury's Lady

30.11.23

In Bramingham Sainsbury's far away

There's a checkout lady we like to pay

For she is interesting, with a mask

And she is perfectly up to the task

Of processing quickly items of food

And generally seems in a chatty mood

The mask is appealing to my brother –

For staunch mask wearing he was another

Who liked to wear one when few others did

In order to keep both nose and mouth hid

Our raid on Sainsbury's includes bottles

She processes whilst wearing goggles

A plastic visor guards her health

As we increase J Sainsbury's wealth

Tesco Helper

3.12.23

The checkout machines in Tesco

Once allowed cash from friend or foe

But now, alas, it's only card

Which makes shopping a bit more hard

Sometimes machine problems arise

And I attempt to catch the eyes

Of the ever-present helper

Wanting them to come right over

My favourite helper is a man

I'm sure he has many a fan

Because he's cheerful and polite

And often he will you invite

To take a bag – as he is tasked

And then he'll say "At least I asked"

If you decide to turn it down

Because you'd brought one into town

He's more attentive than the rest

Of Tesco staff, I like him best

24

The Gospel according to 'Slip End John'

5.12.23

During the pandemic I chanced upon

An extraordinary man near Slip End

I subsequently learned from a friend that his name was John

For an hour he told me why he believed in God

And he seemed to have good reason to do so

His advice to one and all was:

"Be humble and be constructive"

The King

3.1.24

On the 6th of December the King came

To see Luton's people, both white and B.A.M.E.

There was singing and crowds at the Town Hall

And a good time was had by nearly all

Except for one person who threw an egg

Before the King went onto his next leg

Of a journey including Luton's D.A.R.T.

Slightly space-age-like it did look the part

And a Sikh temple which he then opened

With a Sikh soup kitchen he did attend

I caught glimpses of him whilst in the town

To see somebody of such great renown

Was a most special moment in my life

Especially after some recent strife

The Wheelbarrow Man

15.1.24

A man with a wheelbarrow in Loughborough town

Whilst I was still striving to earn my gown

Put down his wheelbarrow half full of cash

And gave me a fiver from out of his stash

To buy from McDonalds a nice burger

I bought and gave him it, not thinking further

He said that they wouldn't take his money

Perhaps choosing me, being young and sunny

I carried on with doctoral studies

Helped in this by a couple of buddies

Later, reflecting on this strange meeting

For remarkableness it takes some beating

Tim Martin

2.1.24

Me and my brother met him once

He shook our hands - he was no dunce

It happened in The White House pub

After we had finished our grub

Up on the book-shelved balcony

We didn't expect him to see

It was a moment that we treasure

Meeting him was such a pleasure

He weren't too grand for a brief natter

Such things as this really do matter

And now his merit's recognised

The King his title has upsized

No longer "Mr", now he's "Sir"

I'm sure his customers concur

That it's a knighthood well deserved

By all the staff who 'spoons have served

Wigmore Wonders

14.1.24

In Lockdown I visited Wigmore Park

In Summer, so I knew it wouldn't get dark

I went on foot and the weather was fine

The total mileage was about nine

It was my first time visiting there

So often I would just stand and stare

Highlights were a lovely horseshoe of trees

And a teenage boy just shooting the breeze

Who offered to do a backflip for me

If I would pay him a five-pound fee

I said I'd give him a single pound

And he did it, landing well on the ground

I gave him the pound and we both were pleased

For the both of us the day had seized

I walked through the park and home I went

The day had most certainly been pleasant

A day of innocent adventure and fun

All whilst enjoying the Lockdown sun

<u>Wilko Man</u>

2.12.23

In Luton's Wilko there's a man

Who oozes kindness like few can

Middle-aged and slightly balding

One wonders if he's found his calling

He's a user of a wheelchair

And has a very friendly air

Though he seems slightly careworn

He does not look like he's forlorn

Instead he often wears a smile

That makes my shopping trip worthwhile

Alas, Wilko is shut right now

And p'r'aps he's made his final bow

But when it re-opens next week

It won't be long before I seek

To see if I can find him there

I hope Wilko for him do care

An angel in a busy mall

With, hopefully, many a pal

Yohan

21.12.23

Playing on the island in Ashton Road
That's not so very far from my abode
With guitar in hand was the kind Yohan
It was the first time that I saw the man
He was very well dressed, he wore a suit
And I came across him along my route

He did seem to have his own religion
Though he appeared to be a Christian
Smiling, happy and full of brotherly love
He almost seemed to be sent from above
He always tells me that Jesus loves me
It seems to me that his soul's most pretty

I think of him now, as a kind of balm
Helping me feel a little bit more calm
After a horrid encounter in town
Thinking of Yohan helps the tears flood down

Printed in Great Britain
by Amazon

41572132R00020